A Quick Word with

BETH MOORE

A Quick Word with

BETH
MOORE

Scriptures & Quotations from
BREAKING FREE

May you be
strengthened with
all power, according to
His glorious might,
for all endurance and
patience, with joy.

Colossians 1:11

We learn to be
victorious only by
surrendering our lives
completely to the
Spirit of God, not by
gritting our teeth
and trying harder.

"I hereby proclaim
freedom for you"—
this is the Lord's
declaration—"to the
sword, to plague,
and to famine!"

Jeremiah 34:17

May the bondage of
mediocre discipleship
never again be acceptable
to us. Christ calls us to a
place of breaking free.
He woos us to a place of
absolute freedom—
the only kind
of freedom that is real.

This is what the
Lord God of Israel says:
"I brought you out of
Egypt and out of the place
of slavery. I delivered you
from the power of Egypt
and the power of all who
oppressed you."

Judges 6:8–9

We would rather God just fix our messes. We don't want to get into the reasons why. But God wants us to know why we continue being oppressed, so that the next time we're in the same situation, we'll make different choices.

He will not
break a bruised reed,
and He will not put out a
smoldering wick, until He
has led justice to victory.
The nations will put their
hope in His name.

Matthew 12:20–21

I feel the Spirit of
God sometimes say to
me: "I understand that
you're not very happy
about this, that you're
scared to death, that you
may be crying over this.
Cry, shake, whatever, but
do My will, Child.
I have victory for you."

The Lord is my
strength and my shield;
my heart trusts in Him,
and I am helped.
Therefore my heart
rejoices, and I praise
Him with my song.

Psalm 28:7

Only God can put the
pieces of our heart back
together again, close up
all the wounds, and bind
them with a porous
bandage that protects
from infection, yet keeps
the heart free to inhale
and exhale love.

I will make known
the Lord's faithful love
and . . . the many good
things He has done for
the house of Israel and
has done for them based
on His compassions and
the abundance of His
faithful love.

Isaiah 63:7

God chooses to heal
or not to heal for His
own reasons. But all His
decisions come from His
love. He cannot love us
any more or less than He
does at this moment.
Whether He chooses to
heal or take us home, His
love remains constant.

They disciplined us
for a short time based on
what seemed good to
them, but He does it for
our benefit, so that we
can share His holiness.

Hebrews 12:10

Sometimes I wonder why God continues to be so faithful. Yes, He is faithful to chastise, or how would we learn from our rebellion? But He is also so compassionate in His comfort.

When the completion
of the time came, God
sent His Son, born of a
woman . . . to redeem
those under the law, so
that we might receive
adoption as sons.

Galatians 4:4–5

God always cares more
for our freedom than
even we do. He initiated
the saving relationship
between the people
and the Liberator.

We who live
are always given over to
death because of Jesus,
so that Jesus' life may
also be revealed in
our mortal flesh.

2 Corinthians 4:11

Life involves change,
and change involves loss.
But every time we suffer
loss, we encounter an
opportunity for it to bring
gain for Jesus' sake by
allowing His life to
be revealed in us.

The High and Exalted
One who lives forever,
whose name is Holy, says
this: "I live in a high and
holy place, and with the
oppressed and lowly of
spirit, to revive the spirit
of the lowly and revive
the heart of the
oppressed."

Isaiah 57:15

Christ came to set the captive free, no matter what kind of yoke binds them. He came to bind up the brokenhearted, no matter what broke the heart. He came to open the eyes of the blind, no matter what veiled their vision.

We all, with unveiled
faces, are reflecting the
glory of the Lord and are
being transformed into
the same image from
glory to glory; this is
from the Lord who
is the Spirit.

2 Corinthians 3:18

A life that glorifies
Christ is not something
we suddenly attain.
As we spend time in
the presence of God,
His glory transforms
us and begins to
radiate from us.

Since you have been
liberated from sin and
become enslaved to God,
you have your fruit, which
results in sanctification—
and the end is eternal life!

Romans 6:22

No matter where you
are on the journey to the
glorifying, liberated life
in Christ, you are His
treasure. He does not
want to take from you.
He wants to give to you
and free you from
any hindrance.

Will not God grant justice to His elect who cry out to Him day and night? Will He delay to help them? I tell you that He will swiftly grant them justice.

Luke 18:7–8

God will sometimes allow
things to get bad enough
that we will be forced
to look up. But victory
always begins with a cry
for help. When we come
to the end of ourselves
and finally cry out
for help, amazing
things happen.

Surely You desire integrity in the inner self, and You teach me wisdom deep within. Purify me with hyssop, and I will be clean; wash me, and I will be whiter than snow.

Psalm 51:6–7

God's truth is not the
only absolute necessity
in our progress toward
complete freedom. Our
truthfulness is a necessity,
as well. A combination
of these two vehicles—
God's truth and our own
truthfulness—will drive
us to our desired
destination.

Everyone who drinks from this water will get thirsty again. But whoever drinks from the water that I will give him will never get thirsty again— ever! In fact, the water I will give him will become a well of water springing up within him for eternal life.

John 4:13–14

We can easily be led
into captivity by seeking
other answers to needs
and desires only God
can meet. Perhaps we
each have experienced an
empty place deep inside
that we tried our best
to ignore or to fill with
something other
than God.

You will keep in
perfect peace the mind
that is dependent on You,
for it is trusting in You.
Trust in the Lord forever,
because in Yah, the Lord,
is an everlasting rock!

Isaiah 26:3–4

Peace comes in
situations that are
completely surrendered
to the sovereign authority
of Christ. When we
finally give up trying to
discover all the whys
and just decide to trust
Him, unexpected peace
washes over us like
a summer rain.

I wait for the Lord;
I wait, and put my hope
in His word. I wait for
the Lord more than
watchmen for the
morning.

We need more than
just a leader on our road
to freedom. We need a
Savior—One who keeps
on saving. Although we
need saving from eternal
separation from God only
once, Christ continues
His saving work in us for
the rest of our lives.

He humbled Himself by
becoming obedient to the
point of death—even to
death on a cross. For this
reason God also highly
exalted Him and gave
Him the name that is
above every name.

Philippians 2:8–9

You may never feel like giving your circumstance, hurt, or loss over to God, but you can choose to submit to Him out of belief and obedience rather than emotion. Obedience is always the mark of authentic surrender to God's authority.

The humble will
have joy after joy in the
Lord, and the poor people
will rejoice in the Holy
One of Israel.

Isaiah 29:19

If I had to define my
relationship with God
by one general statement,
I would tell you that He is
the absolute joy of my life.
I don't just love Him. I
love loving Him. I don't
know any other way to say
it: He works for me.

Then I will make you
a fortified wall of bronze
to this people. They will
fight against you but will
not overcome you, for
I am with you to save
you and deliver you.

Jeremiah 15:20

Do not let the enemy
steal one bit of the victory
God has for you. We must
not allow intimidation or
fear to imprison us in any
area. Remember, Satan
can presume no authority
in your life. He will do his
best to bluff you.
Don't let him.

I will rebuild its
ruins and will set
it up again, so that
those who are left of
mankind may seek
the Lord.

God's expertise is reconstruction. After all, Christ was a carpenter by trade. Nothing has ever been allowed to crumble in a Christian's life or heritage that God can't reconstruct and use.

God is not a man who
lies, or a son of man who
changes His mind. Does
He speak and not act, or
promise and not fulfill?

Numbers 23:19

If we think we've discovered God to be unfaithful, one of three things has happened: 1) we misinterpreted the promise, 2) we missed the answer, or 3) we gave up before God timed His response.

Two blind men
followed Him, shouting,
"Have mercy on us, Son
of David!" When He
entered the house, the
blind men approached
Him, and Jesus said to
them, "Do you believe
that I can do this?"

Matthew 9:27–28

Christ can heal anyone
or perform any wonder,
whether the belief of the
person is great or small.
He isn't asking us to
believe in our ability to
exercise unwavering faith.
He is asking us to believe
that He is able.

Lord, You have heard
the desire of the humble;
You will strengthen their
hearts. You will listen
carefully, doing justice
for the fatherless and the
oppressed, so that men
of the earth may terrify
them no more.

Psalm 10:17—18

Our society looks
on biblical humility as a
sign of weakness. Nothing
could be further from the
truth. Humility takes a
supply of supernatural
strength that comes only
to those who are strong
enough to admit
weakness.

Joshua told the people,
"Consecrate yourselves,
because the Lord will
do wonders among
you tomorrow."

Joshua 3:5

The wonders God
wants to do in all our
tomorrows are prepared
for in our todays.

If you return to Me,
if you remove your
detestable idols from
My presence and do not
waver . . . then the nations
will be blessed by Him
and will pride themselves
in Him.

Jeremiah 4:1–2

Some of the idols in our lives—the things or people we have put in God's place—can take a long time to remove. Some of them have been in those places for years, and only the power of God can make them budge.

He feeds on ashes.
His deceived mind has
led him astray, and he
cannot deliver himself,
or say, "Isn't there a lie
in my right hand?"

Isaiah 44:20

How many times have
I fed on ashes instead of
feasting on the life-giving
Word of God? How many
times has my deluded
heart misled me? How
many times have I tried
to save myself?

Don't worry about anything, but in everything, through prayer and petition with thanksgiving, let your requests be made known to God. And the peace of God, which surpasses every thought, will guard your hearts and your minds in Christ Jesus.

Philippians 4:6–7

To experience a
peace that covers all
circumstances, the
Bible challenges us to
develop active, authentic,
meaty prayer lives. Prayer
with real substance to it—
original thoughts flowing
from a highly individual
heart, personal and
intimate.

This is what the Lord
says: "I will make peace
flow to her like a river,
and the wealth of nations
like a flood; you will nurse
and be carried on her hip,
and bounced on her lap."

Isaiah 66:12

God's Word does not
say we'll have peace like a
pond. To have peace like a
river is to have security
and tranquility even while
meeting many bumps
and unexpected turns
on life's journey.

You caused me to
experience many troubles
and misfortunes, but You
will revive me again. You
will bring me up again,
even from the depths
of the earth.

Psalm 71:20

Worldly philosophy
is forced to minimize
difficulty because it has
no real answers. But you
and I know better than
small-stuff philosophy.
We face a lot of big stuff
out there. Only through
prayer are we washed
in peace.

Be careful that no
one takes you captive
through philosophy and
empty deceit based on
human tradition, based
on the elemental forces
of the world, and not
based on Christ.

Colossians 2:8

Christ came to set the
captive free. Satan comes
to make the free captive.
Christ wants to cut some
binding ropes from our
lives. Satan will want to
use them to tie us
up in knots.

Christ has liberated us
into freedom. Therefore
stand firm and don't
submit again to a
yoke of slavery.

Galatians 5:1

We tend to think of
our generational chains
and hand-me-down
baggage as part of who
we are rather than how
we're bound. We're apt to
consider them part of our
personality rather than a
yoke that's squeezing
abundant life from us.

His master said
to him, "Well done,
good and faithful slave!
You were faithful over
a few things; I will put
you in charge of many
things. Share your
master's joy!"

Matthew 25:21

Christ wants us to share
His happiness, to live
happily ever after.
Until then, He gives us
a sudden splash of
happiness here and there
so we can wet our toes in
what we'll be swimming
in for all of eternity!

One thing I do:
forgetting what is behind
and reaching forward to
what is ahead, I pursue
as my goal the prize
promised by God's
heavenly call in
Christ Jesus.

Philippians 3:13 – 14

God's Word clearly
expresses what a good
and effective teacher the
past can be. But the past
will be a good teacher
only if we will approach it
as a good student, from
the perspective of what
we can gain and how God
can use it for His glory.

I will give them
a heart to know Me,
that I am the Lord.
They will be My people,
and I will be their God
because they will return
to Me with all
their heart.

Jeremiah 24:7

I believe one reason God
requires our cooperation
is that He deeply desires
our involvement with
Him. He created us for
this purpose. Remember,
God's primary purpose in
healing us from our hurts
is to introduce us to new
depths of relationship
with Him.

We must not hide
them from their children,
but must tell a future
generation the praises of
the Lord, His might, and
the wonderful works
He has performed.

Psalm 78:4

Between every
unfaithful generation
and faithful generation is
one person determined to
change. If your dream and
desire for your children
or grandchildren is in
keeping with what you
know of God's will, then
you have the approval of
God to begin acting on it.

Let us be glad, rejoice,
and give Him glory,
because the marriage
of the Lamb has come,
and His wife has
prepared herself.

Revelation 19:7

We cannot make ourselves ready to meet Christ the moment we see Him any more than a woman can be prepared to meet her groom at the altar with three minutes' notice. I don't want to be caught with spiritual curlers in my hair!

You do not want
a sacrifice, or I would
give it; You are not
pleased with a burnt
offering. The sacrifice
pleasing to God is a
broken spirit. God, You
will not despise a broken
and humbled heart.

Psalm 51:16—17

One of the primary
reasons God sent His Son
to this earth was to bring
tender salve and relief to
those whose hearts have
been broken. I believe
that only God can truly
and completely heal
shattered hearts.

I called on Your
name, Yahweh, from the
depths of the Pit. You
hear my plea: Do not
ignore my cry for relief.
You come near when I
call on You; You say:
"Do not be afraid."

Lamentations 3:55–57

Life's way of reacting
to a crushed heart is to
wrap tough sinews of
flesh around it and
promise we'll never let
ourselves get hurt again.
But in keeping love from
going out, we keep love
from coming in. We risk
becoming captives in our
own self-made fortresses.

You rejoice in this,
though now for a short
time you have had to be
distressed by various trials
so that the genuineness of
your faith . . . may result
in praise, glory, and honor
at the revelation of
Jesus Christ.

1 Peter 1:6–7

God does not
minimize the things
that break our hearts.
He left our bare feet on
the hot pavement of earth
so we could grow through
our hurt, not ignore and
refuse to feel our way
through them.

The Lord your God
is testing you to know
whether you love the
Lord your God with
all your heart and
all your soul.

Deuteronomy 13:3

God does not take our
spiritual temperature
under the tongue by the
words we say, nor in our
ear by the impressive
teachings we hear, nor
under our arms by the
service we perform.
God takes our spiritual
temperature straight
from the heart.

As for you,
continue in what
you have learned and
firmly believed, knowing
those from whom
you learned.

2 Timothy 3:14

Let me tell you how
I deal with the "whys"
to which I can't find
answers: I find as many
answers as I can in God's
Word, fill in those blanks,
and trust Him with
the rest.

No one undergoing
a trial should say, "I am
being tempted by God."
For God is not tempted
by evil, and He Himself
doesn't tempt anyone.

James 1:13

In trying to discern
whether God or Satan is
the author of a hardship,
one of your best clues is
whether sin is involved.
God never entices us to
sin, nor does He employ
sin or perversion as a
means of molding us into
the image of Christ.

You could not possibly
do such a thing: to kill
the righteous with the
wicked, treating the
righteous and the wicked
alike. You could not
possibly do that! Won't
the Judge of all the earth
do what is just?

Genesis 18:25

The longer we hold
on to injustices done
against us, the more the
bondage will strangle the
life out of us. Forgiveness
requires our deferring the
responsibility for justice
to Christ and deciding to
be free of the ongoing
burden of bitterness
and blame.

If anyone serves Me,
he must follow Me.
Where I am, there
My servant also will be.
If anyone serves Me,
the Father will
honor him.

John 12:26

Satan tries to draw
us away from God's
authority by making us
think we can be our own
producer and director.
But God did not design
us to boss ourselves.
He formed our psyches
to require authority so
we'd live in the safety
of His careful rule.

Let the evil of the
wicked come to an end,
but establish the
righteous. The One
who examines the
thoughts and emotions
is a righteous God.
My shield is with God,
who saves the upright
in heart.

Psalm 7:9–10

I finally came to the place where I felt more sorry for my perpetrator than I did for myself. I'd rather be the loved and cherished victim than the victimizer. As my nephew used to say when he was little, "Dat dude's in bid trouble."

Arise, cry out in
the night, from the
first watch of the night.
Pour out your heart like
water before the Lord's
presence. Lift up your
hands to Him.

Lamentations 2:19

Christ is never
intimidated by the depth
of our need and the
demonstration of our
weakness. I am so glad
that I don't have to keep
a "stiff upper lip" and set
a good example for others
to follow when I'm
all alone with God
and hurting.

The Lord will make you
the head and not the tail;
you will only move
upward and never
downward if you listen to
the Lord your God's
commands I am giving
you today and are careful
to follow them.

Deuteronomy 28:13

If I follow Christ
through my situation,
I know I can be
victorious. If I blow it
badly or react wrongly,
I can still choose to
follow Him the rest of
the way. It's never too late
to start following His
lead in your crisis.

He has sent Me
for His glory against
the nations who are
plundering you, for
anyone who touches
you touches the pupil
of His eye.

Zechariah 2:8

I've slowly come to trust
God's sovereignty enough
to believe that anyone I
must obey on this earth
had better be careful
with me, or they have
God to answer to!

My goal is to
know Him and the
power of His resurrection
and the fellowship of
His sufferings, being
conformed to
His death.

Philippians 3:10

Few of us escape
betrayal in one way or
another, but will we
choose to fellowship with
Christ in the midst of it,
trusting the sovereignty
of our heavenly Father
who allowed it? Betrayal
can either hurt and hurt.
Or hurt and help. The
choice is up to us.

Jesus said to her,
"I am the resurrection
and the life. The one who
believes in Me, even if
he dies, will live."

John 11:25

Perhaps the most
profound miracle of
all is living through
something we thought
would kill us. And not
just living, but living
abundantly, living
effectively, raised from
living death to
a new life.

Why do you spend
money on what is not
food, and your wages on
what does not satisfy?
Listen carefully to Me,
and eat what is good,
and you will enjoy the
choicest of foods.

Isaiah 55:2

God is leading us
to a land of fulfilled
dreams and victory over
our sin nature, desiring to
bring deep satisfaction
into our hearts. Does this
seem almost too good to
be true? Actually, He's too
good to be false.

Knowing the time,
it is already the hour
for you to wake up
from sleep, for now
our salvation is
nearer than when
we first believed.

Romans 13:11

We were created to give Christ's invisible character a glimpse of visibility. If we grasp the eternal implications of such a destiny, we would want to do anything possible to make sure all hindrances are removed.

In her chamber, the royal daughter is all glorious, her clothing embroidered with gold. In colorful garments she is led to the king; after her, the virgins, her companions, are brought to you. They are led in with gladness and rejoicing; they enter the king's palace.

Psalm 45:13–15

If Satan has convinced you to see yourself as anything less than the handpicked child of the King of kings, if you think anything could happen to steal your royal heritage, if you think you deserve mistreatment or disrespect, may God restore your lost dignity and teach you your true identity.

Go and announce
directly to Jerusalem that
this is what the Lord says:
"I remember the loyalty
of your youth, your love
as a bride—how you
followed Me in the
wilderness, in a land
not sown."

Jeremiah 2:2

A loving bride is willing
to follow her groom to
places that at times may
seem like wilderness. Our
Bridegroom sometimes
leads us to difficult places,
but we can trust Him to
always have purpose in
our stay and never
to forsake us.

We personally had a
death sentence within
ourselves so that we would
not trust in ourselves,
but in God who raises the
dead. He has delivered us
from such a terrible death,
and He will deliver us; we
have placed our hope in
Him that He will deliver
us again.

2 Corinthians 1:9—10

Most people I know who live free have experienced a serious stronghold or hindrance they fought to overcome. I rarely meet people who have come to trust God fully who haven't also painfully confronted the fact that they can't trust themselves.

The Lord is near all
who call out to Him,
all who call out to Him
with integrity. He fulfills
the desires of those who
fear Him; He hears
their cry for help
and saves them.

Psalm 145:18—19

Hearts that are not surrendered to God can seldom be trusted. Until we surrender our hopes and dreams to Christ, we really have very little way of knowing what would fulfill us.

The one who looks
intently into the perfect
law of freedom and
perseveres in it, and is not
a forgetful hearer but
a doer who acts—this
person will be blessed
in what he does.

James 1:25

We want God to
wave a wand over us
and magically remove
every hindrance without
requiring anything of us.
But if God simply waved
a wand over us and broke
every yoke without our
cooperation, we would
soon pick up another.

You have turned things
around, as if the potter
were the same as the clay.
How can what is made
say about its maker,
"He didn't make me"?
How can what is formed
say about the one who
formed it, "He doesn't
understand what
he's doing"?

Isaiah 29:16

Oh, what a disservice
we do when we try to
humanize God by
imagining Him as the
best of humanity rather
than all-together God!
Clay that insists on
acting like the Potter
will inevitably end
up in pieces.

I say then,
walk by the Spirit
and you will not
carry out the desire
of the flesh.

Galatians 5:16

Our liberation is
expressed as a reality
only in the places of our
lives where the free Spirit
of God is released. We are
free when, and only when,
He is in control.

Now may the God
of hope fill you with
all joy and peace in
believing, so that you
may overflow with
hope by the power
of the Holy Spirit.

Romans 15:13

A crucial part of fleshing out our liberation in Christ means allowing Him to fill the empty places in our lives. I'm not talking about a life full of activities. I'm talking about a soul full of Jesus.

During His earthly life,
He offered prayers and
appeals, with loud cries
and tears, to the One who
was able to save Him
from death, and He was
heard because of His
reverence. Though a Son,
He learned obedience
through what He
suffered.

Hebrews 5:7–8

As an earthen vessel,
Jesus had to trust His
Father's will completely.
Although rejection,
suffering, and shame were
part of His experience,
He accepted His
God-given ministry
at every difficult turn
because He trusted
His Father's heart.

Do you not know that
if you offer yourselves to
someone as obedient
slaves, you are slaves of
that one you obey—either
of sin leading to death or
of obedience leading to
righteousness?

Romans 6:16

We have exactly
two options: we can be
slaves to a loving God
or slaves to sin.
Door number three only
exists on *Let's Make a Deal.*

At daybreak, Lord,
You hear my voice;
at daybreak I plead my
case to You and watch
expectantly.

Psalm 5:3

I believe God awakens
us in the morning with
a supernatural ability to
hear from Him. At the
beginning of the day,
we haven't gone the
wrong way yet.

How happy is
the man who has
put his trust in the
Lord and has not
turned to the proud
or to those who
run after lies!

Psalm 40:4

Trusting an invisible God
doesn't come naturally for
us. A trust relationship
grows only by stepping
out in faith and making
the choice to trust. The
ability to believe God
develops most often
through pure experience.

The Lord God will help
Me; therefore I have
not been humiliated;
therefore I have set
My face like flint,
and I know I will not
be put to shame.

Isaiah 50:7

Every day
can bring trouble,
but every day we have a
blessed Troubleshooter.
We must daily set our
faces like flint on the face
of Christ and follow Him
step by step to victory.

Then they cried out
to the Lord in their
trouble; He saved them
from their distress. He
brought them out of
darkness and gloom
and broke their
chains apart.

Psalm 107:13–14

No matter how long
we've walked with God,
we will still have days that
seem dark. In those times,
God tells us to trust in
His name and rely on
who He is. Never will
He hold your hand more
tightly than when He is
leading you through
the dark.

Though the mountains
move and the hills shake,
My love will not be
removed from you and
My covenant of peace
will not be shaken.

Isaiah 54:10

What do we need when the mountains shake, when our hills are removed? Babies die without it. Children must have it. Adults search for it. We'll only find real freedom in a love that will not go away.

Some of you
will rebuild the
ancient ruins; you will
restore the foundations
laid long ago; you will
be called the repairer
of broken walls, the
restorer of streets
where people live.

Isaiah 58:12

The Ancient of Days is
waiting to build a solid
foundation that your
descendants can live on
for years to come if they
choose. He's not asking us
to rebuild ancient ruins
by ourselves. He's simply
asking us to be one of
the tools He uses.

In My Father's house
are many dwelling places;
if not, I would have told
you. I am going away to
prepare a place for you.

John 14:2

All our lives, God retains the strong feelings toward us that infants evoke in their parents because He never has to let us go! He's not rearing us to *leave* home. He's rearing us to *come* home.

Many adversities
come to the one who is
righteous, but the Lord
delivers him from
them all.

Psalm 34:19

God has carefully and
graciously allowed some
of my fears to come
true so that I would
discover that I would
not disintegrate. God
taught me to survive
on His unfailing love.
It wasn't fun, but it was
transforming!

I am the Alpha
and the Omega, the
First and the Last, the
Beginning and
the End.

Revelation 22:13

Oh, God, awaken our souls to see that You are not just what we need, but what we want. Yes, our life's protection, but also our heart's affection. Yes, our soul's salvation, but also our heart's exhilaration. You are the fulfillment of our chief desire in all of life.

Yes, Lord,
we wait for You
in the path of
Your judgments.
Our desire is for
Your name and
renown.

Isaiah 26:8

Any time we glorify God,
we are displays of His
splendor. But right now
I want to paint a portrait
of a life that truly
withholds nothing from
God, a life through which
God does something only
He can do.

The one who believes
in Me, as the Scripture
has said, will have streams
of living water flow from
deep within him.

John 7:38

No matter how long
we struggle, God is not
giving up on us. Even if
we've drained all the
human resources
around us dry, He is
our inexhaustible well
of living water.

No discipline seems enjoyable at the time, but painful. Later on, however, it yields the fruit of peace and righteousness to those who have been trained by it.

Hebrews 12:11

The measures God
takes to woo us to liberty
may be excruciating at
times, but they are often
more powerful evidences
of His unfailing love than
all the obvious blessings
we could expound. Few
truly know the unfailing
love of God like the
captive set free.

Stephen, filled by
the Holy Spirit, gazed
into heaven. He saw
God's glory, with Jesus
standing at the right
hand of God.

Acts 7:55

Never once in
my youth did I hear
clear teaching about the
Spirit-filled life. Perhaps
this is the reason why
I refuse to shut up
about it now.

Whatever you do,
do it enthusiastically,
as something done for
the Lord and not for men,
knowing that you will
receive the reward of
an inheritance from
the Lord—you serve
the Lord Christ.

Colossians 3:23–24

Whenever the enemy tries to use your physical lineage against you, use your spiritual lineage against him! As a child of God and a joint heir with Christ, refuse the enemy a single inch of the ground you are taking back.

He put everything
under His feet and
appointed Him as head
over everything for the
church, which is His body,
the fullness of the One
who fills all things
in every way.

Ephesians 1:22—23

When you make a daily practice of inviting His love to fill your hollow places and make sure you are not hindering the process, God will begin to satisfy you more than a double cheeseburger!

To those who are
perishing, the message
of the cross is foolishness,
but to us who are being
saved, it is God's power.

1 Corinthians 1:18

The healthiest Christians
you will ever meet are
not those with perfect
physiques but those who
take a daily dose of
God's Word and choose
to believe it works.

The precepts of
the Lord are right,
making the heart glad;
the commandment of
the Lord is radiant,
making the eyes
light up.

Psalm 19:8

God made sure to inscribe His love for you in His Word so you'd never have to wait for a phone call. You can hear Him tell you He loves you every single time you open the Word.

Let all who
seek You rejoice
and be glad in You;
let those who love
Your salvation
continually say,
"The Lord is great!"

Psalm 40:16

I fear we may have become so legalistic that we've dropped the word *happy* from our religious vocabulary. Allow me to get this off my chest once and for all. Sometimes God just plain makes me happy! Call me immature, but picture me smiling.

Father, I desire those You have given Me to be with Me where I am. Then they will see My glory, which You have given Me because You loved Me before the world's foundation.

John 17:24

I think heaven will be
heaven because He will
be there, but He thinks
heaven will be heaven
because you will be there.

God's love was revealed
among us in this way:
God sent His One and
Only Son into the world
so that we might live
through Him.

1 John 4:9

No one has ever done
more to show you that
you were unloved than
God has done to show
you that you *are* loved.

Your statutes are
the theme of my song
during my earthly life.
I remember Your name
in the night, Lord, and
I keep Your law.
This is my practice:
I obey Your precepts.

Psalm 119:54—56

We're all looking
for a quick fix, but God
is after lasting change—
lifestyle Christianity.
To possess a steadfast
mind is to practice a
steadfast mind.

Grace has come
from the Lord our God
to preserve a remnant
for us and give us a stake
in His holy place. Even
in our slavery, God has
given us new life and
light to our eyes.

Ezra 9:8

Have you been among
the living dead?
The stone's been rolled
away. Resurrection life
awaits you. Will you
continue to sit in a dark
tomb, or will you walk
into the light of
resurrection life?
Lazarus, come forth!

On that day the
remnant of Israel and
the survivors of the house
of Jacob will no longer
depend on the one who
struck them, but they will
faithfully depend on
the Lord, the Holy
One of Israel.

Isaiah 10:20

We don't become victors
by conquering the enemy
but by surrendering
to Christ. We don't
become victors by our
independence from
the enemy but by our
dependence on God.

Watch out, brothers, so
that there won't be in any
of you an evil, unbelieving
heart that departs from
the living God. But
encourage each other
daily, while it is still called
today, so that none of
you is hardened by
sin's deception.

Hebrews 3:12–13

Once we are willing to
see the sin involved in our
stronghold and agree with
God through confession,
we begin to see the lies
surrounding us. Tearing
down the lies that are
wallpapering our minds
causes the prison door
to swing open.

I see a different law
in the parts of my body,
waging war against the
law of my mind and
taking me prisoner to the
law of sin in the parts
of my body.

Romans 7:23

We possess the mind
of Christ, but we still have
the full capacity to think
with the mind of the
flesh. We are mentally
bilingual, you might say.
But we will think with the
mental language we
practice most.

Therefore,
my dear brothers,
be steadfast, immovable,
always excelling in the
Lord's work, knowing that
your labor in the Lord
is not in vain.

1 Corinthians 15:58

More than you seek to defeat the enemy, seek his foe! More than you seek victory, seek the Victor! You'll never be more beautiful to God than when He can look down and see you hanging on to Him for dear life!

The training of the
body has a limited
benefit, but godliness is
beneficial in every way,
since it holds promise
for the present life and
also for the life to come.

1 Timothy 4:8

Godliness is not
perfection. If you are
striving daily to give God
your heart and mind and
are sensitive to sin,
I'd call you godly.

Who among them can
declare this, and tell us
the former things?
Let them present their
witnesses to vindicate
themselves so that people
may hear and say,
"It is true."

Isaiah 43:9

We are never more
beautiful portrayals of
mortals who know and
believe God than when
others can look at our
lives, hear our
testimonies, and say,
"It is true." That's
what it means to be
living proof.

I have come down
to rescue them from the
power of the Egyptians
and to bring them from
that land to a good and
spacious land, a land
flowing with milk
and honey.

Exodus 3:8

God never misses
a single groan or cry of
His children. He always
has a rescue mission
planned. When the time
is right, God will move in
behalf of His children.

We demolish arguments
and every high-minded
thing that is raised up
against the knowledge
of God, taking every
thought captive to the
obedience of Christ.

2 Corinthians 10:4–5

You and I have been
controlled and held
prisoner by destructive,
negative, and misleading
thoughts for too long.
Through the power of the
Holy Spirit, we can take
our thoughts prisoner
instead.

Then all your
people will be righteous;
they will possess the land
forever; they are the
branch I planted, the
work of My hands, so that
I may be glorified.

If you love Him
more today than you did
when you began, then this
difficult road has been
worth traveling.